Copyright ©2021 Charlene A. Ryan

All rights reserved. No part of this book may be reproduced or used in any manner whatsoever without written permission of the copyright owner except for the use of brief quotations in a book review.

First paperback edition September 2021

ISBN (paperback): 978-1-954041-06-6
ISBN (hardback): 978-1-954041-07-3

Published by Creative Sound Press
www.creativesoundpress.com
publishing@creativesoundpress.com

All book and cover art created with oil on canvas by Charlene A. Ryan.
All rights reserved.

creativesoundpress.com

# Up and Down Sounds

**Charlene A. Ryan**

For Matthew, Aiden, Audrey Anna, and Amelia Claire.
May your ups always be greater than your downs.

# How to use this book

Each page is a unique work of art designed to represent higher and lower sounds. The images at the beginning of the book rise and fall in seemingly random arrangements. As the book progresses, so do the shapes, which begin to resemble those found in traditional musical notation. The artwork provides an aesthetic impetus for engaging children in vocal exploration and forms the building blocks for reading music notation. Encourage children to imagine the sounds that they hear in the images and to think about how the sounds within a given piece of artwork might differ from each other. Ask them to consider what vocal sounds they could use to sing the patterns — oohs, aahs, ums, las, dahs, and loos (and any other syllables they want to try!). And when you've exhausted the book's possibilities, have the children create their own artwork to sing, consolidating their conceptual understanding of pitch and notation, their developing singing skills, and their aural and visual creativity.

Climb the track higher...

and then go down...

Go over the bump...

and now the hump...

Go round and round....

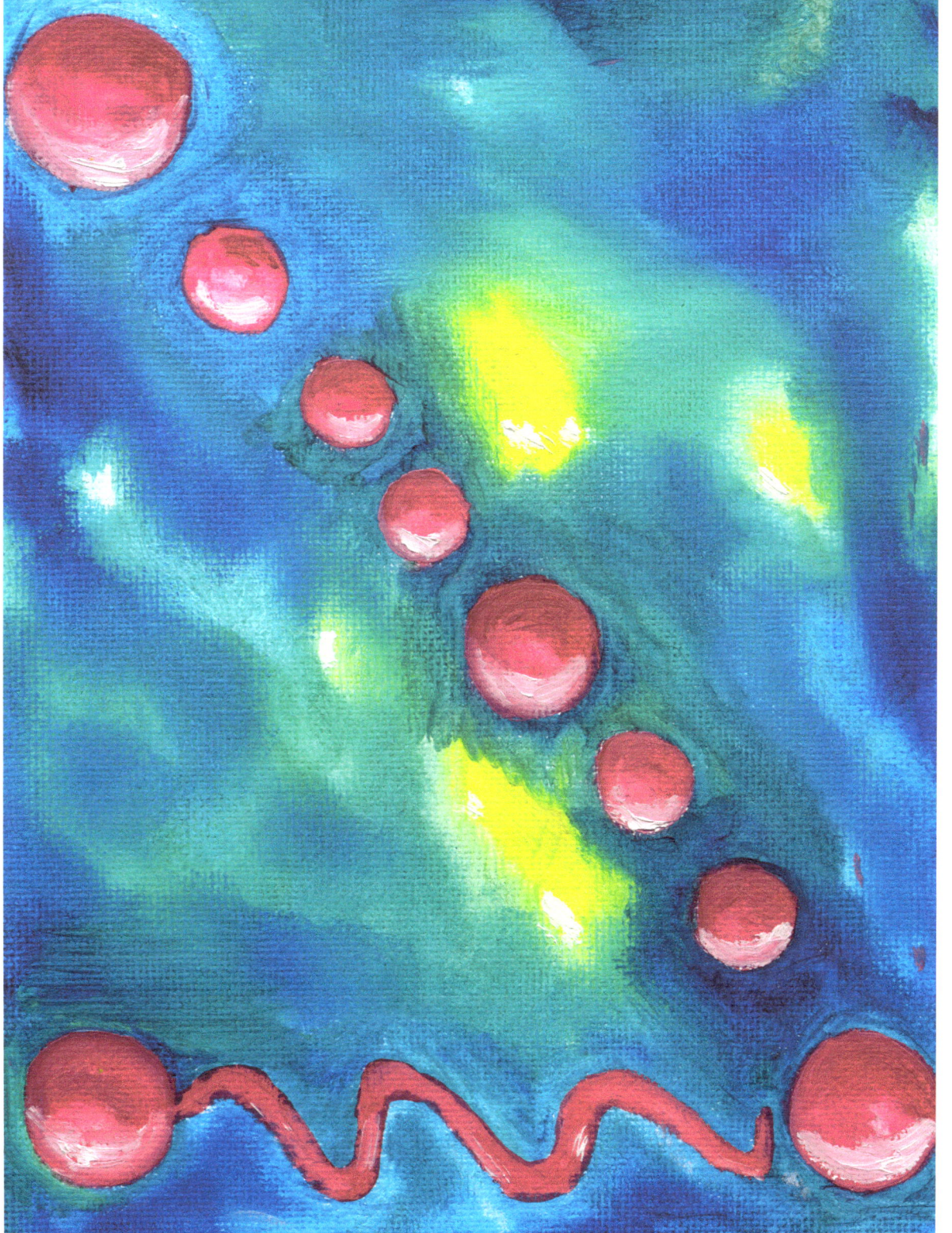

and up then down...

Go one by one...

and hold it some...

Now roll and roll...

over hills and knolls...

Smoothly flow...

then loop de loop...

Glide high then low...

Which way to go?

Floating higher...

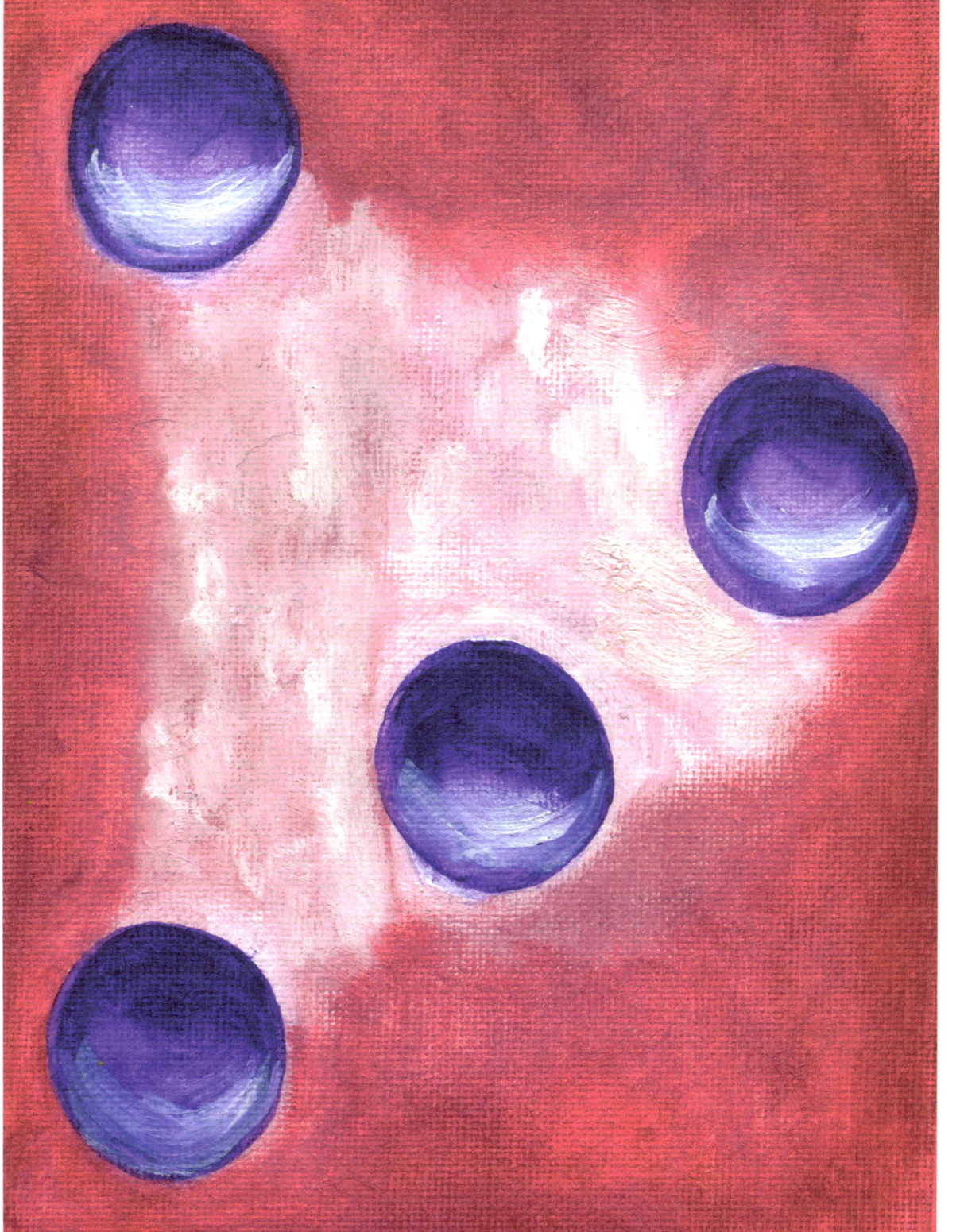

Leap up, then lower...

Far apart...

Close together...

Double the middle....

Leap up, step a little...

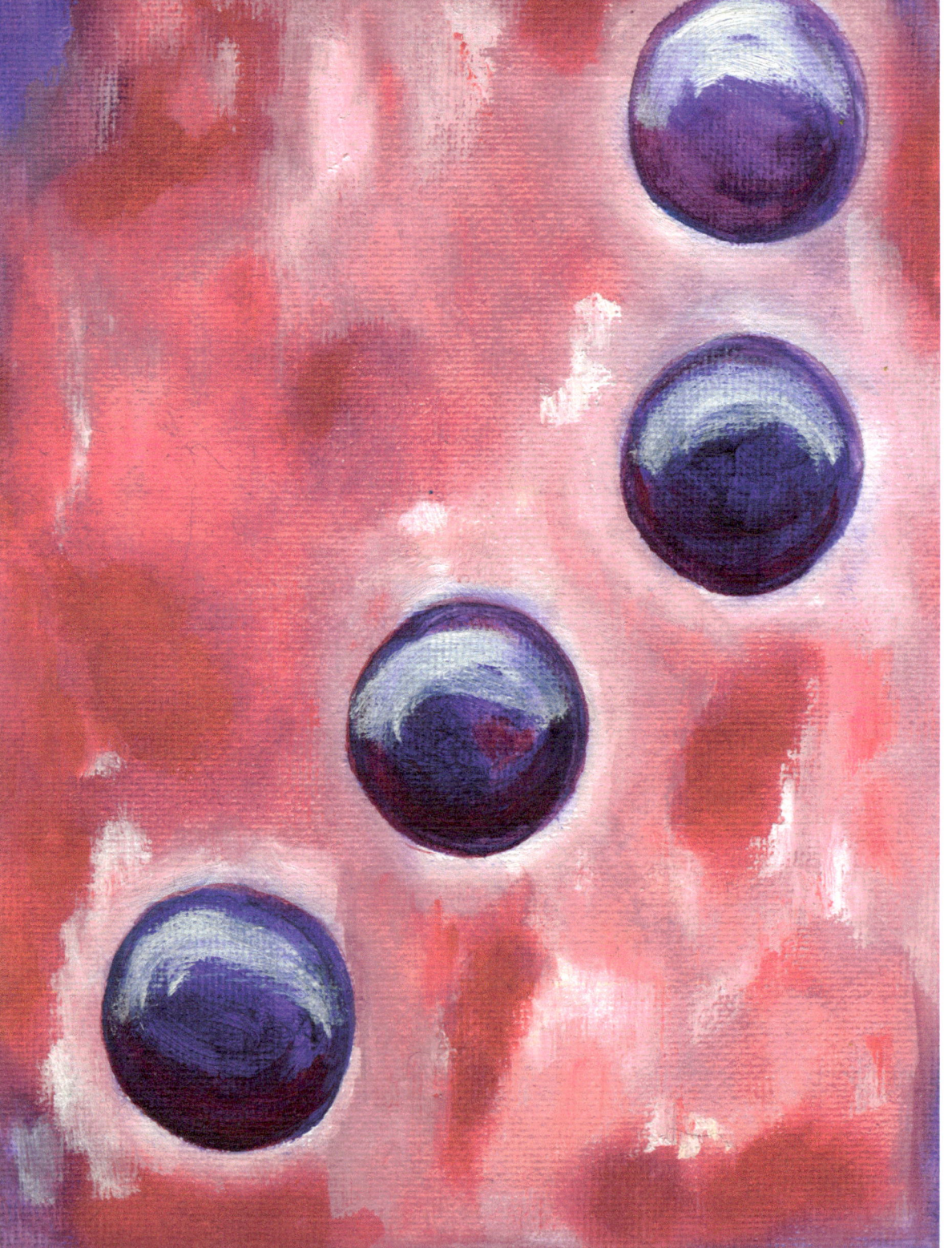

Repeat the bottom...

Rise and return...

Pivot a little....

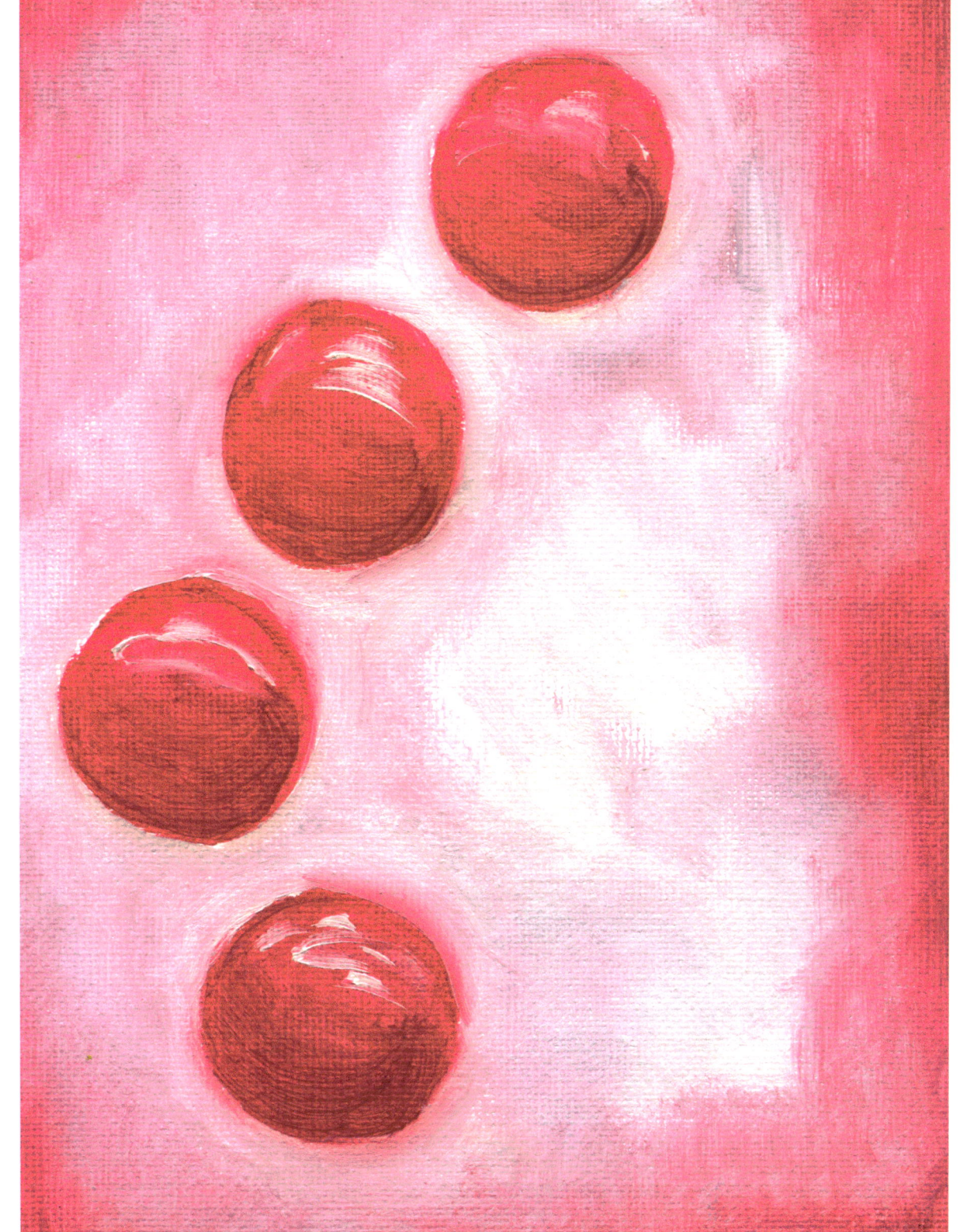

down around and adjourn.

Charlene A. Ryan is a musician, painter, writer, and mom. She has spent most of her life behind an instrument and in front of an audience of one kind or another.

Other books by Charlene include:

Sections of Sound
Big and Small Sounds
Hannabelle's Butterflies
Katherine Lost

To learn more about Charlene and her work, visit www.charlenearyan.com

www.ingramcontent.com/pod-product-compliance
Lightning Source LLC
Chambersburg PA
CBHW041100070526
44579CB00002B/21